SOCIAL PROGRESS AND SUSTAINABILITY

Shelter • Safety • Literacy • Health • Freedom • Environment

EURASIA

reword by **Michael Green,**
ecutive Director, Social Progress Imperative

By Don Rauf

SOCIAL PROGRESS AND SUSTAINABILITY

THE SERIES:

AFRICA: NORTHERN AND EASTERN

AFRICA: MIDDLE, WESTERN, AND SOUTHERN

EAST ASIA AND THE PACIFIC

EUROPE

EURASIA

NEAR EAST

SOUTH AND CENTRAL ASIA

NORTH AMERICA

CENTRAL AMERICA AND THE CARIBBEAN

SOUTH AMERICA

Social Progress and Sustainability

Shelter • Safety • Literacy • Health • Freedom • Environment

Eurasia

Don Rauf

Foreword by
Michael Green
Executive Director, Social Progress Imperative

MASON CREST

Mason Crest
450 Parkway Drive, Suite D
Broomall, PA 19008
www.masoncrest.com

Printed and bound in the United States of America

First printing
9 8 7 6 5 4 3 2 1

Series ISBN: 978-1-4222-3490-7
Hardcover ISBN: 978-1-4222-3495-2
ebook ISBN: 978-1-4222-8390-5

Library of Congress Cataloging-in-Publication Data

Names: Rauf, Don, author.
Title: Eurasia/by Don Rauf; foreword by Michael Green, executive director, Social Progress Imperative.
Description: Broomall, PA : Mason Crest, [2017] | Series: Social progress and sustainability | Includes index.
Identifiers: LCCN 2016007604| ISBN 9781422234952 (hardback) | ISBN 9781422234907 (series) | ISBN 9781422283905 (ebook)
Subjects: LCSH: Social indicators—Eurasia—Juvenile literature. | Eurasia—Social conditions—Juvenile literature. | Eurasia—Economic conditions—Juvenile literature.
Classification: LCC HN380.7.A85 R39 2017 | DDC 306.095—dc23
LC record available at http://lccn.loc.gov/2016007604

Developed and Produced by Print Matters Productions, Inc. (www.printmattersinc.com)

Project Editor: David Andrews
Design: Bill Madrid, Madrid Design
Copy Editor: Laura Daly

Note on Statistics:
All social progress statistics, except where noted, are used by courtesy of the Social Progress Imperative and reflect 2015 ratings.

CONTENTS

Foreword: Social Progress around the Globe by Michael Green 6

Introduction: Social Progress in Eurasia 11

1 **Basic Human Needs** **23**

2 **Foundations of Well-being** **33**

3 **Opportunity** **45**

4 **Eurasian Countries at a Glance** **57**

Conclusion 71

Glossary 73

Index 77

Resources 79

KEY ICONS TO LOOK FOR:

Text-Dependent Questions: These questions send the reader back to the text for more careful attention to the evidence presented there.

Words to Understand: These words with their easy-to-understand definitions will increase the reader's understanding of the text, while building vocabulary skills.

Series Glossary of Key Terms: This back-of-the book glossary contains terminology used throughout this series. Words found here increase the reader's ability to read and comprehend higher-level books and articles in this field.

Research Projects: Readers are pointed toward areas of further inquiry connected to each chapter. Suggestions are provided for projects that encourage deeper research and analysis.

Sidebars: This boxed material within the main text allows readers to build knowledge, gain insights, explore possibilities, and broaden their perspectives by weaving together additional information to provide realistic and holistic perspectives.

SOCIAL PROGRESS AROUND THE GLOBE

Michael Green

How do you measure the success of a country? It's not as easy as you might think. Americans are used to thinking of their country as the best in the world, but what does "best" actually mean? For a long time, the United States performed better than any other country in terms of the sheer size of its economy, and bigger was considered better. Yet China caught up with the United States in 2014 and now has a larger overall economy.

What about average wealth? The United States does far better than China here but not as well as several countries in Europe and the Middle East.

Most of us would like to be richer, but is money really what we care about? Is wealth really how we want to measure the success of countries—or cities, neighborhoods, families, and individuals? Would you really want to be rich if it meant not having access to the World Wide Web, or suffering a painful disease, or not being safe when you walked near your home?

Using money to compare societies has a long history, including the invention in the 1930s of an economic measurement called gross domestic product (GDP). Basically, GDP for the United States "measures the output of goods and services produced by labor and property located within the U.S. during a given time period." The concept of GDP was actually created by the economist Simon Kuznets for use by the federal government. Using measures like GDP to guide national economic policies helped pull the United States out of the Great Depression and helped Europe and Japan recover after World War II. As they say in business school, if you can measure it, you can manage it.

Many positive activities contribute to GDP, such as
- Building schools and roads
- Growing crops and raising livestock
- Providing medical care

More and more experts, however, are seeing that we may need another way to measure the success of a nation.

Other kinds of activities increase a country's GDP, but are these signs that a country is moving in a positive direction?
- Building and maintaining larger prisons for more inmates
- Cleaning up after hurricanes or other natural disasters
- Buying alcohol and illegal drugs
- Maintaining ecologically unsustainable use of water, harvesting of trees, or catching of fish

GDP also does not address inequality. A few people could become extraordinarily wealthy, while the rest of a country is plunged into poverty and hunger, but this wouldn't be reflected in the GDP.

In the turbulent 1960s, Robert F. Kennedy, the attorney general of the United States and brother of President John F. Kennedy, famously said of GDP during a 1968 address to students at the University of Kansas: "It counts napalm and counts nuclear warheads and armored cars for the police to fight the riots in our cities ... [but] the gross national product does not allow for the health of our children.... [I]t measures everything in short, except that which makes life worthwhile."

For countries like the United States that already have large or strong economies, it is not clear that simply making the economy larger will improve human welfare. Developed countries struggle with issues like obesity, diabetes, crime, and environmental challenges. Increasingly, even poorer countries are struggling with these same issues.

Noting the difficulties that many countries experience as they grow wealthier (such as increased crime and obesity), people around the world have begun to wonder: What if we measure the things we really care about directly, rather than assuming that greater GDP will mean improvement in everything we care about? Is that even possible?

The good news is that it is. There is a new way to think about prosperity, one that does not depend on measuring economic activity using traditional tools like GDP.

Advocates of the "Beyond GDP" movement, people ranging from university professors to leaders of businesses, from politicians to religious leaders, are calling for more attention to directly measuring things we all care about, such as hunger, homelessness, disease, and unsafe water.

One of the new tools that has been developed is called the Social Progress Index (SPI), and it is the data from this index that is featured in this series of books, Social Progress and Sustainability.

The SPI has been created to measure and advance social progress outcomes at a fine level of detail in communities of different sizes and at different levels of wealth. This means that we can compare the performance of very different countries using one standard set of measurements, to get a sense of how well different countries perform compared to each other. The index measures how the different parts of society, including governments, businesses, not-for-profits, social entrepreneurs, universities, and colleges, work together to improve human welfare. Similarly, it does not strictly measure the actions taken in a particular place. Instead, it measures the outcomes in a place.

The SPI begins by defining what it means to be a good society, structured around three fundamental themes:

- Do people have the basic needs for survival: food, water, shelter, and safety?
- Do people have the building blocks of a better future: education, information, health, and sustainable ecosystems?

- Do people have a chance to fulfill their dreams and aspirations by having rights and freedom of choice, without discrimination, with access to the cutting edge of human knowledge?

The Social Progress Index is published each year, using the best available data for all the countries covered. You can explore the data on our website at http://socialprogressimperative. org. The data for this series of books is from our 2015 index, which covered 133 countries. Countries that do not appear in the 2015 index did not have the right data available to be included.

A few examples will help illustrate how overall Social Progress Index scores compare to measures of economic productivity (for example, GDP per capita), and also how countries can differ on specific lenses of social performance.

- The United States (6th for GDP per capita, 16th for SPI overall) ranks 6th for Shelter but 68th in Health and Wellness, because of factors such as obesity and death from heart disease.
- South Africa (62nd for GDP per capita, 63rd for SPI) ranks 44th in Access to Information and Communications but only 114th in Health and Wellness, because of factors such as relatively short life expectancy and obesity.
- India (93rd for GDP per capita, 101st for SPI) ranks 70th in Personal Rights but only 128th in Tolerance and Inclusion, because of factors such as low tolerance for different religions and low tolerance for homosexuals.
- China (66th for GDP per capita, 92nd for SPI) ranks 58th in Shelter but 84th in Water and Sanitation, because of factors such as access to piped water.
- Brazil (55th for GDP per capita, 42nd for SPI) ranks 61st in Nutrition and Basic Medical Care but only 122nd in Personal Safety, because of factors such as a high homicide rate.

The Social Progress Index focuses on outcomes. Politicians can boast that the government has spent millions on feeding the hungry; the SPI measures how well fed people really are. Businesses can boast investing money in their operations or how many hours their employees have volunteered in the community; the SPI measures actual literacy rates and access to the Internet. Legislators and administrators might focus on how much a country spends on health care; the SPI measures how long and how healthily people live. The index doesn't measure whether countries have passed laws against discrimination; it measures whether people experience discrimination. And so on.

- What if your family measured its success only by the amount of money it brought in but ignored the health and education of members of the family?
- What if a neighborhood focused only on the happiness of the majority while discriminating against one family because they were different?
- What if a country focused on building fast cars but was unable to provide clean water and air?

The Social Progress Index can also be adapted to measure human well-being in areas smaller than a whole country.

- A Social Progress Index for the Amazon region of Brazil, home to 24 million people and covering one of the world's most precious environmental assets, shows how 800 different municipalities compare. A map of that region shows where needs are greatest and is informing a development strategy for the region that balances the interests of people and the planet. Nonprofits, businesses, and governments in Brazil are now using this data to improve the lives of the people living in the Amazon region.
- The European Commission—the governmental body that manages the European Union—is using the Social Progress Index to compare the performance of multiple regions in each of 28 countries and to inform development strategies.
- We envision a future where the Social Progress Index will be used by communities of different sizes around the world to measure how well they are performing and to help guide governments, businesses, and nonprofits to make better choices about what they focus on improving, including learning lessons from other communities of similar size and wealth that may be performing better on some fronts. Even in the United States subnational social progress indexes are underway to help direct equitable growth for communities.

The Social Progress Index is intended to be used along with economic measurements such as GDP, which have been effective in guiding decisions that have lifted hundreds of millions of people out of abject poverty. But it is designed to let countries go even further, not just making economies larger but helping them devote resources to where they will improve social progress the most. The vision of my organization, the Social Progress Imperative, which created the Social Progress Index, is that in the future the Social Progress Index will be considered alongside GDP when people make decisions about how to invest money and time.

Imagine if we could measure what charities and volunteers really contribute to our societies. Imagine if businesses competed based on their whole contribution to society—not just economic, but social and environmental. Imagine if our politicians were held accountable for how much they made people's lives better, in real, tangible ways. Imagine if everyone, everywhere, woke up thinking about how their community performed on social progress and about what they could do to make it better.

Note on Text:
While Michael Green wrote the foreword and data is from the 2015 Social Progress Index, the rest of the text is not by Michael Green or the Social Progress Imperative.

This political map shows the countries of the region discussed in this book.

SOCIAL PROGRESS IN EURASIA

Eurasia Today

In geographic terms, Eurasia has been defined as the area that makes up both the continents of Europe and Asia. In this volume, Eurasia is defined as Russia, Eastern European countries that have been associated with Russia, and Turkey, which geographically straddles both continents. In this region, Russia dominates. Russia is the biggest country in the world, and it also has one of the largest economies.

The main religion in Russia, Armenia, Belarus, Georgia, Macedonia, Moldova, Montenegro, Serbia, and Ukraine is Christianity. The Muslim religion predominates in Albania, Azerbaijan, Bosnia and Herzegovina, and Turkey. Most of these countries have been more aligned with Eastern Europe than Western Europe, and a distinguishing factor for these countries is that they are all not in the European Union. The alliances, however, have been changing over the years. A few countries—Albania, Bosnia and Herzegovina, Kosovo, and Turkey— are potential candidates for the European Union. At the end of May 2014, the leaders of Russia, Belarus, and Kazakhstan signed a treaty establishing their own regional trading bloc called the Eurasian Economic Union (EEU). Other members include Armenia, Belarus, and Kyrgyzstan. The EEU sees potential to enlarge with Georgia, Moldova, and Tajikistan, as well as Iran, Syria, and Turkey. Ukraine is also possible, but the recent conflict between Russia and Ukraine may have dimmed those prospects.

Almost all of the countries in Eurasia rank lower than most European nations on the Social Progress Index (SPI). Some have relatively strong foundations for nutrition, basic medical care, and education, but they are weaker in areas concerning personal rights. Even with nutrition and medical care being fairly sound, the countries in this region do not score well when it comes to overall health and wellness. Eurasia as a whole has a higher SPI ranking than Africa and South and Central Asia, but it is lower than South America, Central America, and North America.

Moldova is one of the poorest countries in Eurasia. When the Soviet Union (USSR) collapsed in 1991, Moldova became an independent republic. It has high foreign debt and high unemployment. The average gross domestic product (GDP) per capita is just $4,521. Compare that to the United States, where GDP per capita is about $53,000. The country, however, overperforms on the SPI. Even though this is a relatively new country, it benefits from systems set up under the Soviet Union, especially education and basic health services.

The economy of Russia relies heavily on oil and gas, so when world prices go down, as they have over the past few years, the economy of Russia sinks as well. The 2016 Index of Economic Freedom reported that "Russia's prospects for long-term, diversified, sustainable economic growth remain bleak. There is no efficiently functioning legal framework, and government continues to interfere in the private sector through myriad state-owned enterprises. Corruption pervades the economy and continues to erode trust in the government."

Russia also has a poor environmental record. In 2015, the *Moscow Times* wrote that the country's environmental problems date back to "breakneck Soviet industrialization in the early 20th century, when whole regions were blighted in

A young student and his mother shop for school supplies in Moldova, where incomes are low but life is good.

the rush to modernize the economy." In the 21st century, the Russian cities of Dzerzhinsk and Norilsk have been among the 10 most polluted places on earth. Dzerzhinsk produced chemical weapons, and Norilsk has been a major mining town for more than 80 years.

Instability in Eurasia has increased since fighting between Ukraine and Russia broke out in 2014. The conflict began when Russia annexed Crimea, a region that was part of Ukraine at the time but that is claimed by both Ukraine and Russia, after separatist groups in Russian-speaking eastern and southern

Russian Black Sea Fleet officers stand in line in Nakhimov Square ahead of a parade in Sevastopol's streets as part of celebrations of the first anniversary of the reunification of Crimea with the Russian Federation.

Ukraine voted to secede over attempts to bring Ukraine into an association with the European Union. Following this referendum, Russian military forces crossed the border into the Crimean peninsula and gained control of key locations, including government buildings, airports, and military bases. The area is now administered by Russia as the Republic of Crimea and the federal city of Sevastopol.

The United States and the European Union (EU) have argued that the vote to secede was illegitimate and that its outcome will not be recognized. As Crimea rejoined Russia, other parts of eastern Ukraine came under dispute. Pro-Russian citizens there have called for rejoining Russia as well, and skirmishes have led to the deaths of about 9,000 people since the spring of 2014. Because of Russia's annexation of Crimea and backing of separatists in eastern Ukraine, the United States and the EU imposed sanctions (trade barriers and restrictions on financial transactions) on Russia. These sanctions have had a serious effect on the Russian economy.

After the Ukrainian government agreed to give more autonomy to this region, the fighting subsided. In the summer of 2015, Ukraine president Petro Poroshenko called for Russian forces to get out of Ukrainian territory. An uneasy truce seems to be in place, but the underlying reasons for the tension have not been addressed.

Another area of concern for both Europe and Eurasia is the continuing crisis caused by the record numbers of refugees who have been fleeing Syria, Iraq, and North Africa. While Europe has been giving refuge to hundreds of thousands of refugees, Russia has refused to join any plan to assist refugees. Russia also has been at odds with Europe and the United States over the civil war in Syria. Russian president Vladimir Putin has backed Syria's government let by Bashar al-Assad, sending the Russian military, especially air support, to join the fight against opposition groups, while the EU and the United States have been pushing to have him removed before any ceasefire between the Syrian government and rebel forces can be negotiated. As part of its involvement in Syria, Russia announced plans in September 2015 to establish a military base in Syria to defeat Muslim extremists known as the Islamic State of Iraq and the Levant (ISIL or ISIS). Turkey has joined the United States and other allies in the fight against ISIS. The Migration Policy Institute says that Turkey hosts the world's largest community of Syrians displaced by the ongoing conflict in their country with more than 1.7 million living in Turkey.

History of Eurasia

Eurasia's history is largely about its largest country and its influence in this area. Like most countries, Russia began with different migrating tribes who eventually settled and developed into kingdoms. Over time, different communities of people came together to form the nation of Russia. Starting in the late 800s, Kiev grew to become the center of a trade route that connected Scandinavia to Constantinople. The empire built around Kiev was called Kievan Rus, and it prospered for 300 years. In the late 10th century, Vladimir I was an influential leader in ancient Russia. He chose Eastern Byzantine Christianity as the national religion. In 988 he brought together the people of Kiev along the banks of the Dnieper River and had them all baptized. Under his rule, architecture and literacy flourished.

In 1237 the Mongols, led by the grandson of Genghis Khan, Batu Khan, invaded Kievan Rus. The Mongols formed a confederation called the Tatar state, or the Empire of the Golden Horde. By the 14th century, northeastern cities in Russia gained more influence, and Moscow became Russia's spiritual capital. In time, the people of Moscow challenged Tatar rule, and by 1480 Moscow was able to free itself from the Tatars. Under the rule of Ivan the Great, Moscow began to take control of other cities. His grandson, Ivan the Terrible, became Tsar of all Russia. (The word *tsar* is from "Caesar.") Ivan was so named for his ruthlessness, and he expanded the empire to include Siberia. Under his rule, peasants were assigned to a master, and a system of serfdom was established.

In 1582 the Russian army lost a war with Poland, Lithuania, and Sweden, forcing Ivan the Terrible to give up regions in the north. As he grew older, he grew more volatile. He was known for mood shifts, unreliability, and egocentricity. One day, in a rage, he struck his son and heir, Ivan, with a metal rod, killing him. He left Russia economically and politically weakened.

Other tsars came to power, but it was the Romanov dynasty that proved to be longest lasting, ruling from 1613 until 1825. In 1696 Peter of the Romanov family initiated extensive reforms designed to make Russia a great nation. Compared to other European countries at this time, Russia was seriously underdeveloped. Peter modernized the army, created a navy, supported science, and developed more commerce and industry. He simplified the Russian alphabet and introduced Russia to its first newspaper. He brought European culture to Russia, but he was also very strict and maintained a harsh class system that kept peasants as virtual slaves. He extended Russian territories to include Estonia, Latvia, and Finland. His successful battles against Turkey gained Russia passage to the Black Sea. At great material and human cost, Peter moved the capital from Moscow and built St. Petersburg.

The next important leader of Russia was Catherine the Great. She was an avid supporter of the arts and pushed forward an era of building, architecture, libraries, journals, and academies. She called for reform in the land so that every man could be declared equal. She expanded Russian territory into Poland and fought against the Ottoman Empire, which was centered in present-day Turkey. Through a treaty with the Ottoman Empire in 1774, Russia acquired more land and strengthened its foothold on the Black Sea. She also took over the Crimean peninsula. The early 1800s were marked by Napoleon's failed attempt

A painting from the State Central Navy Museum in St. Petersburg shows the 1877 capture of a Turkish warship on the Black Sea.

to conquer Russia, and as the century progressed, the absolute control of the tsars began to loosen. In the 1820s, military officers made a failed attempt for a constitutional monarchy. The century brought an age of industrialization, and while Emperor Alexander II abolished serfdom, it had little effect.

In the late 1800s and then into the early 1900s, Russia was battered from war. During World War I, Russia suffered demoralizing defeats, food shortages, and economic ruin. These conditions paved the way for a workers' revolt. Vladimir Lenin became the champion of working people's rights and welfare. In 1917 open elections were held. Under Lenin's administration, the Russian Empire was dissolved and the Soviet Union was formed. In time, the new government confiscated and nationalized all industry and natural resources, but for a brief period in the 1920s, Lenin introduced a type of capitalism-oriented policy and the region experienced relative prosperity. Culture flourished, and the era produced a unique Russian art movement. Under Lenin's administration, the Soviet Union annexed Armenia, Georgia, and Azerbaijan. Any hope of a market economy was obliterated when Lenin died and Joseph Stalin took control. Stalin ruled as a dictator and personal freedoms were strictly controlled. All arts, literature, and education were dictated by the state and many artists were directed to create art glorifying Stalin. Stalin conducted a nationwide campaign to destroy churches and religious property. To maintain his control, he killed millions. Stalin infamously said: "One death is a tragedy; one million is a statistic."

After Stalin's death, repressive government controls were slowly dismantled, but the next decades under the rule of Nikita Khrushchev, Leonid Brezhnev, and others were marred by stagnation and poor economic policies. Personal freedoms were slow in coming. Real change came in 1985, when Mikhail Gorbachev became the leader of the Soviet Union and introduced a period of glasnost (openness) and perestroika (restructuring). In 1989 the first open elections since 1917 were held. By 1991 the Soviet Union was breaking up. Azerbaijan, Latvia, Lithuania, and Estonia had declared their independence. Albania, Belarus, and Ukraine also broke away from the Soviet Union. Czechoslovakia and Poland had rid themselves of Soviet influence. Georgia had transformed itself into a functional democracy with a market-oriented economy. Around this same time and in a similar way, Yugoslavia was breaking up, leading to the formation of Bosnia and Herzegovina, Serbia, and Montenegro.

By January 1992 the Soviet Union ceased to exist, and the Russian flag was again flying over the Kremlin, the seat of Russian government. Through the 1990s, Russia rapidly transformed from a state-run economy to one run on capitalist principles and privatization. This "shock therapy" economic plan, however, sent Russia into a period of great economic hardship, with the rich becoming even richer and many people being plunged into poverty. Vladimir Putin came to power in 1999, and since that time the Russian economy has grown—Russia's poverty rate, gross domestic product, and average salaries have all improved. He has also been accused of media interference, secret money deals, and hostile foreign policies.

While Russia was a great cultural power in the north, Turkey, with its predominantly Muslim culture, developed into a powerful cultural and economic force in the south. In the 4th century, Christianity had a strong influence in the region. At this time, the Roman emperor Constantine converted the Roman Empire to Christianity. He built his seat of power in largely Christian Byzantium, which was renamed Constantinople and today is Istanbul. For 1,100 years this Byzantine Empire controlled the region. With the start of Islam in the year 610, a shift began. This year marks the first revelation to the prophet Muhammad at the age of 40. Turkish nomadic tribes converted to Islam in the 8th and 9th centuries. In 1453 the Muslim Ottoman Empire dominated the region and lasted for hundreds of years. From the 17th to 19th centuries, Turkey and Russia fought each other in a series of wars, as Russia expanded its territory and pushed its way to the Black Sea. In 1914 Turkey entered World War I on the side of the Germans and the Austro-Hungarian Empire.

Christian Armenians who lived within the territory were considered to be "infidels" by the Muslim Turks. Turks began to view Armenians as the enemy who would fight against Turkey to gain independence. In 1915 Turkey began a large-scale execution of Armenians in the east. Slaughter, starvation, and death claimed the lives of 300,000 to 1.5 million Armenians at this time. The

Armenians visit the Tsitsernakaberd memorial in Yerevan where the centennial of the Armenian Genocide was observed.

Ottomans, however, lost in World War I and surrendered in 1918. In May 1918 the republic of Armenia was founded—95 percent of the population is Christian. Relations between Turkey and Armenia have been strained, but in 2001 a Turkish Armenian Reconciliation Commission was formed to help the two nations improve relations. The Ottoman Empire lasted until 1924, when Mustafa Kemal Atatürk abolished it and established a secular government that is not influenced by religion. Russia and Turkey have inched toward improved relations in recent years—Russia became Turkey's number-two trading partner in 2013. In 2012 Russia and Turkey agreed on visa-free travel for their citizens.

An ethnic Albanian refugee holds a baby while resting in a warehouse where Kosovo refugees found temporary shelter in Kukes, Albania.

CHAPTER 1

BASIC HUMAN NEEDS

Words to Understand

Alcoholism: an addiction to the consumption of alcohol or the mental illness and compulsive behavior resulting from alcohol dependency.

Housing stock: the houses and other places to live in a town, country, area, etc.

Mortality rate: a measure of the number of deaths in an area usually within the span of a year.

Preventive care: care given to prevent illnesses or diseases. This includes check-ups, counseling, screenings, and education.

Privatization: the transfer of ownership, property, or business from the government to the private sector (the part of the national economy that is not under direct government control).

When it comes to meeting the basic human needs for health care and nutrition, Eurasia performs well, but it ranks lower than Europe, the United States, and Canada. Russia performs very well on providing its people with nutrition and basic medical care, scoring just a couple points lower than the top countries in Europe (Iceland, Finland, Norway, and Germany). Most people in Russia have enough to eat and that all citizens have a right to free health care, although the quality of public health care is lower than in most developed countries. Also, the high rates of smoking and **alcoholism** are major health concerns in Russia.

Belarus, Moldova, Russia, and Ukraine are among the top six countries in the world for alcohol consumption. Belarus claims the number-one spot—on average, residents here consume 17.5 liters (about 4.6 gallons) of alcohol a year. The World Health Organization (WHO) discovered that alcohol played a role in about one out of three deaths in Belarus.

Russia also scores low in the area of personal safety. In 2015 the Overseas Security Advisory Council (OSAC) reported that violent crime, including incidents backed by organized crime, is not uncommon in Russia. OSAC has found that auto theft is also common.

Nations that developed under Communist rule generally follow a philosophy that government should provide for the basic needs of their people,

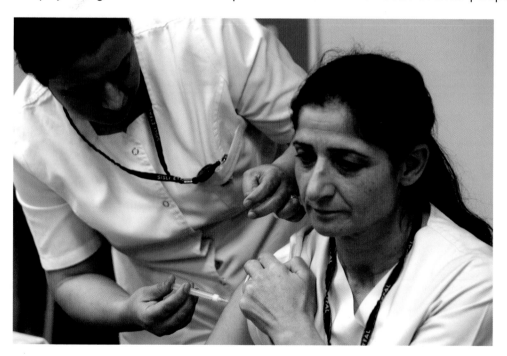

A Turkish nurse in Istanbul administers swine flu vaccine to a patient.

and that includes health care. Belarus has health care that is affordable and readily available. Georgia has a privatized system of health care, but individuals who live below the poverty line have their health care provided by private insurers but paid for from public funds. Old deteriorating hospitals and clinics are slowly being replaced with new facilities. In the Communist era, Armenia enjoyed one of the best health care systems of all the Soviet republics, according to the World Health Organization. Today, a large portion of health care expenditures comes out of the consumer pocket, and fewer people can afford adequate health care. Turkey also gets high marks for providing basic nutrition and health care. Turkey's Ministry of Health is responsible for the delivery of state-run health services, from **preventive care** to hospital operations. Those Turkish citizens who can afford it can pay for a growing number of private health care services.

Dealing with Alcoholism in Russia

There's a Russian proverb: "Vodka is our enemy, so we'll utterly consume it!" And that has been Russia's problem. About 20 million people are alcoholics in Russia, and the country is trying to put the cork back in the bottle when it comes to alcohol abuse. In 2012 the government banned alcohol advertising on television, radio, the Internet, public transportation, billboards, and in print media. Moscow has prohibited sales of spirits and other strong alcohol at night. Higher taxes on alcohol have also been introduced to try to curb rampant alcohol abuse. In a country where many people reportedly drink vodka for breakfast, programs to stop alcoholism have been difficult to establish. People have tried to introduce systems similar to Alcoholics Anonymous, but they have met with resistance. An article in *The Atlantic* magazine pointed out that many in Russia distrust the self-help movement, often because of the perception of it as a religious cult invading the country. The primary treatment plan in Russia has been using a type of psychiatry called coding, which is intended to create a subconscious aversion to alcohol. The Russian government has seemed divided on how to approach alcohol use. It has recognized that alcohol reduces productivity, but it also brings in large amounts of revenue. In the 1970s, alcohol accounted for a third of government revenues. Although Vladimir Putin has criticized excessive drinking, Russia has yet to come up with a comprehensive plan to battle widespread alcoholism.

Health is improving for babies and their mothers in Bosnia and Herzegovina.

Around the globe, the number of child and maternal deaths has been decreasing over the past two decades. The Institute for Health Metrics and Evaluation found that child deaths have been cut in half since 1990, and maternal deaths have dropped by almost a quarter. Eurasia is no different. Russia's infant **mortality rate** has been improving, according to the Centers for Disease Control and Prevention. In 2015 the CIA *World Factbook* showed that there were about seven deaths of infants under one year old in a given year per 1,000 live births in the same year. In 1990, that number was about 18. The World Bank estimated 25 deaths of mothers per 100,000 live births in Russia in 2015. Compare that to Turkey, where the number is 16 per 100,000, and Bosnia and Herzegovina, where it is a low 11 per 100,000. Georgia, however, has one of the worst maternal death rates in the region, at 36 per 100,000. The CIA *World Factbook* also reported that infant deaths per 1,000 live births is at about 7 in Russia, 6 in Serbia, almost 13 in Moldova, and more than 16 in Georgia. The United Nations Data Retrieval System has also found that Georgia has a high death rate for infants—it was three times the European rate between 2010 and 2015. Many factors can endanger an infant's life. Babies that are born preterm can be weak and have trouble surviving. Birth defects, sudden infant death syndrome, maternal health complications, and unintentional injuries can lead to infant death. Proper health care and knowledge at the time of delivery can help babies survive. Dr. John Pardalos is a pediatrician from Columbia, Missouri, who has volunteered in Georgia. He found that a major cause for these deaths may be an inability to establish clear airways in the first five minutes of a baby's life. Programs that train Georgian doctors on how to establish proper breathing in newborns may help improve this problem, according to Dr. Pardalos.

The Eurasian Housing Problem

Having a good quality of life means having a roof over your head, and for Russians finding affordable housing can be a challenge. In 2013 the *Moscow Times* said that saving up to buy an apartment remains a major challenge for most Russians because housing there is the least affordable in Europe. President Putin has been pushing initiatives for more affordable housing, and a spring 2015 issue of *Russia Insider* reported that Russia is in the middle of a housing boom. Russia is known for its cold winters. In Moscow a vast subterranean network of pipes delivers heavily subsidized heat to every home for just a few dollars a month. Other

Retired Albanian men sit together outside an apartment complex in Berat. Affordable housing is in short supply in the country.

regions in Eurasia struggle with housing as well. Habitat for Humanity (habitat. org) indicated that the latest existing **housing stock** in Serbia is insufficient to meet housing needs. Bosnia and Herzegovina was part of the former Yugoslavia and suffered much destruction and damage of homes in the civil wars of the 1990s. Currently, reconstruction of the existing housing stock is the pressing problem in the country. Adequate affordable housing has been an ongoing issue in Belarus, Albania, and Georgia. A 2010 Gallup poll revealed that 4 out of 10 people in Georgia said they didn't have enough money for adequate housing.

Homes for All: The Sudden Privatization of Armenia's Housing

Mikhail Gorbachev became general secretary of the Communist Party of the Soviet Union in March 1985 and introduced new freedoms that led to the breakup of the Soviet Union. After Armenia declared its independence from the Soviet Union in 1991, the new republic went through the most radical housing privatization of all European and Eurasian countries, according to Habitat for Humanity. Basically, about 46 percent of all housing stock that was owned by the state was handed over to the tenants free of charge between 1991 and 1999. Armenia is now called a "super home-ownership" state. By 2000, 96 percent of Armenian housing stock was privatized. The problem has been that many residents are cash poor, and they struggle to maintain their newly owned properties. Also, existing housing has been deteriorating because of poor maintenance. A devastating earthquake in northern Armenia in 1988 destroyed a large portion of housing, and that area is still being rebuilt. Habitat for Humanity has stated that Armenia lacks an overall strategy to develop and maintain adequate housing. Nonprofit groups such as Habitat for Humanity are assisting the country in building better homes. Armenian citizen Gagik Babajanyan said, "For many years my family has been living in the wet and dark basement of our half-built house without any necessary living conditions." Because of a nonprofit group dedicated to providing affordable homes, Gagik now has a completed home for his family.

Water, Water Everywhere, and Only Some to Drink

Most homes throughout Eurasia have access to water. The problem is, not all of it is safe to drink. Some studies have found that about one-fourth of Russia's water is unsafe for human consumption. Tourists are continually warned to drink only bottled water. In Belarus drinking water is often of poor quality because of high iron content. About 15 percent of the population there lacks access to piped water and sanitation. Georgia has a very strong record in providing drinkable water and proper sanitation facilities, according to the World Health Organization. In Tbilisi, Georgia's capital, the water source is pure, but the pipes are older and often have mineral or bacterial buildup.

View of the so-called Tbilisi Sea, Georgia, an artificial lake that serves as a reservoir.

Text-Dependent Questions

1. What is one of the biggest health-related problems facing the people of Russia, Belarus, Moldova, and Ukraine?
2. What is a positive factor for citizens of Russia regarding medical care that helps all people in this country?
3. Which country in Eurasia has one of the highest maternal and infant death rates?
4. Why is Armenia called a "super home-ownership" state?
5. Is housing affordable in Russia?

Research Project

Many areas in Eurasia are in need of decent housing. Nonprofit groups such as Habitat for Humanity try to help by sending volunteers who build homes. Write a summary of three programs that are building affordable homes in Eurasia and how they achieve their goals.

Macedonian high school graduates dance at the main square in the Macedonian capital Skopje.

CHAPTER 2

FOUNDATIONS OF WELL-BEING

Words to Understand

Censorship: government control of the media—books and newspapers, TV and radio, movies and theater—in order to prevent certain ideas from being spread.

Ecosystem: the interaction between all living things—plants, animals, and microscopic organisms—in a particular place or area and their environment, which includes the air, water, and soil.

Industrialization: introduction of industries to a region or country—for example, when an economy goes from being based on agriculture to manufacturing.

Primary education: generally, basic education for children (usually ages 5 to 11), including reading, writing, and basic math. For most countries, primary education is mandatory. Also called elementary education.

Secondary education: generally, education past the primary level. In developed countries, it is usually mandatory.

Education is a means for individuals to empower themselves and improve their lives. Russia scores high under the category Access to Basic Knowledge on the Social Progress Index. The literacy rate in the country is close to 100 percent. Russia shows an appreciation for education every September 1, officially called the "Day of Knowledge." It is a holiday marking the beginning of the school year. Teachers and pupils assemble on this day to present songs, poems, and plays to inspire students about the year ahead. Every school ceremony ends with a girl from the first grade placed on the shoulder of a boy in the senior year of school. She is given a bell, and as the boy walks before the crowd, the young girl rings the bell, marking the beginning of the new school year.

Most children in Russia stay in the same school for their **primary** and **secondary education**. The school will teach children ages 7 to 18, from the first to the 11th grade levels. The first four years are called elementary school, the next five years are junior high school, and the next two years are senior high school. Students are typically graded on a scale of 2 to 5, with 5 being the top grade. In the 11th grade, students take centralized exams that measure their knowledge in important subjects, such as Russian language and literature, math, foreign languages, and natural sciences. Universities use these test scores to evaluate students for college admission.

Armenian pupils sit in class during a lesson.

Compared to most countries in Europe, Moldova, Macedonia, and Bosnia and Herzegovina have lower rates of primary school enrollment. Still, the enrollment stands at more than 85 percent. Turkey has shown some relative

Turkey's Lower Numbers in High School Enrollment

Mustafa Kemal Atatürk formed the independent republic of Turkey in 1923, and one of his policies was to start a government system of education designed to create a skilled working class. The education system has been a battleground between religious conservatives and secularists. Secularists believe in the separation between government and religion, and that religion should be kept out of the schools. Religious conservatives want to see more religious education in the schools. In recent years in Turkey, there has been a shift away from secularism with the rise of a religious lower and middle class. Since 2010 Turkey has seen a 73 percent increase in the number of religious vocational schools, known as *imam-hatip*, according to an article in the *New York Times*. These schools provide a general academic curriculum, but they also instruct students in Islamic teachings. Most of the religious training is based on Sunni Islam, the religion's largest branch. Many students are finding themselves placed in these religious vocational schools, even if they do not have the religious education. The European Court of Human Rights had ruled that Turkey violated the rights of its minorities because its mandatory religious and ethics classes were based on Sunni Islam and did not take into account other religions. Under new laws students can leave the traditional school track after just four years and enter a system of apprenticeship and vocational training. These factors may be leading to lower secondary school enrollment. According to *World Education News & Reviews*, women in Turkey are already 9 percent less likely to complete high school compared to men. Under new laws, parents may withdraw their children from school after the first four years and homeschool them. The fear is that a growing number of conservatives and parents in rural areas may prevent their daughters from attending any school after the first four years.

weakness, with 74 percent of children of the appropriate age enrolled in secondary school. UNICEF reported that Armenia has taken great strides to achieve universal primary school enrollment, but the nation has high dropout rates and low secondary school completion rates.

Access to Communication

People throughout the world are now able to more easily communicate via mobile, or cell, phones, and the countries of Eurasia consistently have cell phone coverage. The Information and Communication Technology (ICT) Development Index, published by the United Nations International Telecommunication Union (itu.int), rates countries according to their level of access to, use of, and skills in using information and communication technology. In 2014 the nations that showed the most dynamic improvement included Belarus, Bosnia and Herzegovina, and Georgia, mostly because they've enhanced their wireless broadband connections. Still, some of the countries have more restrictions on Internet access compared to Europe. Roskomsvoboda, a Russian organization that advocates free Internet access, has said that the Russian Internet has been developing freely and spontaneously, but the Russian government has been pushing to boost its regulatory grip over the Internet and mass media. The government has claimed that it needs to protect the population from harmful information. Laws in Russia and other Eurasian countries allow for the blocking of websites that promote extremism, suicide, harm to children, or illegal drugs. Russia has blocked sites that called for protests over the ongoing crisis in Ukraine. Belarus may have one of the worst reputations for Internet **censorship**. Reporters Without Borders (rsf.org) listed Belarus as an Internet enemy in 2006,

The Internet Party of Ukraine advocates elimination of bureaucracy, free computer courses, and a simplified tax code. Shown above, its leader, "Darth Vader," holds a campaign event before parliamentary elections.

2007, and 2008. When the Belarus economy took a dive in December 2014, the government blocked access to dozens of independent websites that published news on the growing financial trouble.

Longevity in Eurasia

Life expectancy in this part of the world is lower compared to Europe and the United States. The average life span for a Russian is just over 70 years. It's 72 in Belarus, 71 in Ukraine, and about 69 in Moldova. Certain areas perform better: life expectancy is about 75 years in Turkey and Serbia, 76 in Bosnia and Herzegovina, and 77 in Albania. Compare these numbers to the United States, where life expectancy on average is close to 79, and France, where the average is about 82. American men have a 1 in 11 chance of dying before age 55, but for Russian men, those odds rise to 1 in 4. The areas with lower longevity averages have been hard hit with alcohol abuse. More than half of Russians smoke as well, and more than one-quarter are obese. An article in the *Wall Street Journal* ranked Serbia number one in the world for cigarettes sold per capita. Turkey has many smokers as well. A Gallup poll estimated that half the population may smoke, although government measures to ban smoking advertising and smoking in public places may help reduce the number of smokers. While obesity is less of a problem, in Turkey over 17 percent of the population is now considered excessively overweight. In Turkey, the world's 17th-biggest economy, the number of people treated for diabetes has gone up at least 90 percent since 2000. Ukraine, Belarus, and Russia are among the top 25 countries in the world for high suicide rates. In Ukraine, most of the suicides are of members of the military,

Elderly couples dance with children at the central office of the state palace of weddings in Chisinau, Moldova.

where suicides account for up to 50% of all deaths. Heavy alcohol use has triggered more suicides in Russia and Ukraine.

It's Not Easy Being Green in Eurasia

Overall, Eurasia's environmental record is not very strong. Pollution has been one of the largest man-made contributors to premature deaths throughout

A century of oil production and negligence have left the Republic of Azerbaijan on the brink of environmental disaster. Current environmental problems include air, water, and soil. Shown above, oil pumps at sunset in Sabungli, Azerbaijan.

the world. This area went through a period of rapid **industrialization** in the 20th century with little or no regard for the environment. Some scientists have dubbed the Soviet destruction of **ecosystems** as "ecocide"—meaning intentionally killing off the natural environment. In the 1990s, after the breakup of the Soviet Union, Russia categorized 40 percent of Russian territory as under high or moderately high ecological stress. Russia's Federal Service for Hydrometeorology and Environmental Monitoring reported in the spring of 2015 that over one-third of the Russian population lives in the 57 percent of Russian cities that have high or extremely high levels of air pollution. Some estimate that up to three-quarters of Russian surface water is polluted. In today's Russia, the government has some constraints on pollution. The Federal Service for Supervising Natural Resources serves as environmental watchdog, penalizing those businesses that pollute beyond the set limits, but the *Moscow Times* reported that many Russian polluters evade huge fines. Many former republics of the Soviet Union, such as Armenia, Belarus, and Georgia, are also heavily polluted. Throughout Eurasia there appears to be low ecological awareness and education among citizens. While Serbia faces problems with pollution as well, it has one of the highest ratings in the world for maintaining biodiversity.

A woman cultivates tomato plants in central Serbia, where nature is healthy.

Text-Dependent Questions

1. Russia's Day of Knowledge demonstrates the value that the country places on what?
2. Why is education so important to the health of a country?
3. What has been one of the largest man-made contributors to premature deaths in the world?
4. While the lack of the right nutrition has led to increased mortality, a health issue that is almost the opposite has increased deaths worldwide. What is this modern health problem that is causing more deaths?

Research Project

Find out the details on at least three programs in Eurasia that are helping to reduce pollution. Check with Greenpeace or other organizations that may have information about recycling and other programs that decrease pollution and waste.

Thousands of Turkish citizens rally in Istanbul to protest a government crackdown on environmental activists.

CHAPTER 3

OPPORTUNITY

Words to Understand

Defamation: the action of damaging the good reputation of someone; slander or libel.

Democratize: to change the way of running a government or organization so that the people in it are more equal and can share in making decisions; to make democratic.

Extremism: the holding of extreme political or religious views; fanaticism.

Hooliganism: disruptive or unlawful behavior such as rioting, bullying, and vandalism.

Parliament: a group of people who are responsible for making the laws in some kinds of government.

Trafficking: dealing or trading in something illegal.

Whistle-blowing: exposing information or activities within an organization that are seen as illegal, unethical, or wrong.

One measure of social progress in a country is the amount of freedom an individual has. These liberties include freedom of speech, freedom of choice, and freedom of movement—to live and work where one chooses. Overall, Eurasia ranks lower in personal rights and freedoms compared to Europe, the United States, Canada, and many countries in South America.

When it comes to personal rights, Russia scores especially low on the Social Progress Index. Freedom House (freedomhouse.org), a US-based nongovernmental organization that conducts research on political freedom and human rights, downgraded Russia in 2004 from a nation that was "partly free" to one that is "not free" and it has remained that way as of 2015. Belarus and Azerbaijan face similar problems. In September 2015, a journalist who reported on Azerbaijan government corruption was sentenced to seven and a half years in prison. Freedom House has highlighted President Vladimir Putin's concentration of political authority, increased intimidation of the media, and politicization of the country's law enforcement system. The Russian constitution provides for freedom of speech and freedom of the press. Freedom House has stated that Russian officials have used the country's politicized and corrupt court system to harass the few remaining independent journalists who dare to criticize widespread abuses by the authorities, especially under Vladimir Putin's presidency. In 2012, for example, a number of government critics—including journalists, ordinary citizens, and **whistle-blowing** government workers—were charged with **defamation**, **extremism**, and other offenses in an effort to limit their activities.

Since the breakup of the Soviet Union, Russia has had free elections. Putin has been the leader of Russia since 2000, but critics call the government a "managed democracy." Opposing voices are often suppressed. In February 2015, Boris Nemtsov, a vocal opponent of Putin, was gunned down in front of the Kremlin. Suspects have been arrested, and while his death is under investigation and Putin has not been accused, some say that he created an atmosphere that allowed the assassination to happen.

People taking part in rallies that have not been officially permitted can be heavily fined. Henry Hale, a professor of political science at Indiana University in Bloomington, has written that Putin's highly restrictive campaign laws effectively prevent opposition parties from countering the pro-Putin coverage on the nightly news. GOLOS, an independent monitoring organization, has cited thousands of voting abuses—from ballot stuffing to vote rigging. Still, Putin legitimately appears to be popular with a large number of people in Russia. Under his rule, the country has prospered, and the middle class has expanded. He has established himself as the strong protector of the country, and few alternative leaders have been able to gain attention.

Russian President Vladimir Putin is very popular in his country.

Freedom House has found that freedom of religion is supported unevenly in Russia, with preference given to Orthodox Christianity. With the collapse of communism, there has been a religious and cultural revival. Russia has struggled with anti-Semitism, or prejudice against Jews. A museum of Jewish history and culture, however, opened in Moscow in 2012.

Academic freedom is generally respected, and Russia has a high regard for advanced education. In fact, the Organization for Economic Co-operation and Development (OECD) declared Russia to be the most educated country in the world.

The largest nation in the world ranks low, however, when it comes to tolerance of immigrants. Thousands rallied in November 2013 against migrants, whom they accuse of pushing up crime rates and taking jobs. After the USSR dissolved, there was an increase in tolerance of homosexuality and improved gay rights. Gay life in Russia today is in the process of being more accepted, but the movement has met with resistance. A 2015 Associated Press-NORC Center for Public Affairs Research survey found that Russians' tolerance of gays has plummeted in recent years, with 51 percent saying they would not want a gay neighbor. The Orthodox Church in Russia has firmly opposed homosexuality.

Georgia, Moldova, and Ukraine have struggled to **democratize** and become part of Europe in recent years, but they face strong resistance from Russia and antidemocratic elements within their borders. Freedom House has declared Albania, Armenia, Georgia, Macedonia, Moldova, Bosnia and Herzegovina, Turkey, and Ukraine as partly free, based on maintaining some political rights

Moscow police arrest lesbian, gay, bisexual, and transgender rights activists during a gay pride parade.

and civil liberties. On the positive side, Turkey has made constitutional reforms that include limiting the death penalty, lifting restrictions on public rallies, and allowing broadcasts in Kurdish. More recently, in 2015, freedoms have seemed to erode. Turkey's government is using its control over media to limit public debate about government actions and punish journalists and media owners who dispute government claims. Serbia is the only country in Eurasia categorized as "free." All of these countries have maintained relations with

Riot police hold back protesters after a Turkish police raid of opposition television stations.

A Punk Band Challenges Putin

An arrest of a punk rock feminist protest band in 2012 spotlighted the limits of freedom of expression in today's Russia. Founded in 2011 in Moscow, Pussy Riot writes and performs songs about feminism, LGBT rights, and their opposition to Vladimir Putin. They usually wear brightly colored dresses and tights, with their faces masked. The band has had 11 members, but 3 of them, Maria Alyokhina, Nadezhda Tolokonnikova, and Yekaterina Samutsevich, were arrested in February 2012 after taking part in a performance at Moscow's Cathedral of Christ the Savior protesting the Orthodox Church's support of Putin. They were convicted of hooliganism motivated by religious hatred, and each was sentenced to two years in prison (although Samutsevich's sentence was later dropped). Putin defended the prison terms, saying that the women "undermined the moral foundations" of the nation. Many artists and government officials in the West defended their actions as artistic expression and freedom of speech and thought the punishment was too severe. They were released in December 2013 after serving 21 months.

Riot police detain Pussy Riot feminist punk group members during a protest action in front of Zamosvoretsky district court, Moscow, Russia.

Tourists stroll in Belgrade, Serbia's most popular tourism destination.

the European Union and aligned themselves with European ideals for personal rights and freedom.

What Serbia Is Doing Right

As the only country labeled as "free" in Eurasia by Freedom House, Serbia is doing something right to help people maintain personal liberties (in spite of, or possibly because of, its history of supporting ethnic cleansing in the 1990s—over which its

A woman casts her ballot at the polling station in the central Serbian city of Uzice.

then leader Radovan Karadzic was sentenced to genocide by a UN court). Now, Serbia has free elections and a multiparty system. The press is free, and the constitution guarantees freedom of religion. Serbian civil society organizations have a solid record of promoting human rights and anticorruption efforts. In September 2015 in Belgrade, Serbian authorities gave official permission for a pride parade in support of LGBT (lesbian, gay, bisexual, and transgender) rights. Women make up 34 percent of the **parliament**. A 2009 law on gender equality provides a range of protections in employment, health, education, and politics. Serbia still faces challenges—Freedom House points out that domestic violence remains a serious problem. Unemployment hovers at 25 percent. Serbia is a destination country for the **trafficking** of men, women, and children.

Text-Dependent Questions

1. Russia has elections, but it is not considered to be a free country, according to Freedom House. Why isn't it considered "free"?
2. What do the Eurasian countries that have the most personal freedoms have in common?
3. Which country in Eurasia has the most freedom, according to Freedom House?
4. Although President Putin is criticized for his tight grip on the Russian government, he remains popular. What is a reason for his popularity?
5. Personal rights improved for most people in Eurasia after what event?

Research Project

Turkey is considered partly free, according to the independent watchdog association Freedom House. It has many policies in place that make it a free country, including separation of church and state, elections, and constitutional guarantees of press freedom and freedom of expression. In recent years, however, some of those freedoms have been under threat. Write a report summarizing some of the freedoms that Turkey has upheld and how freedoms are being threatened.

A father carrying his son on his shoulders walks in front of the Arch of Triumph, which is decorated with the flags of Moldova and Georgia, in Chisinau, Moldova, as the capital city celebrates its 575th anniversary.

CHAPTER 4

EURASIAN COUNTRIES AT A GLANCE

ALBANIA

QUICK STATS

Population: 3,029,278 (July 2015 est.)
Urban Population: 57.4% of total population (2015)
Comparative Size: slightly smaller than Maryland
Gross Domestic Product (per capita): $11,400 (2014 est.)
Gross Domestic Product (by sector): agriculture 22.6%, industry 15.1%, services 62.4%
Government: parliamentary democracy
Languages: Albanian 98.8% (official: derived from Tosk dialect), Greek 0.5%, other 0.6% (including Macedonian, Roma, Vlach, Turkish, Italian, and Serbo-Croatian), unspecified 0.1% (2011 est.)

SOCIAL PROGRESS SNAPSHOT

Social Progress Index: 68.19 (+7.19 above/below 61 world average)
Basic Human Needs: 80.71 (+12.38 above/below 68.33 world average)
Foundations of Well-being: 73.64 (+7.19 above/below 66.45 world average)
Opportunity: 50.23 (+2.00 above/below 48.23 world average)

Albania declared its independence from the Ottoman Empire in 1912 but was conquered by Italy (1939) and occupied by Germany (1943). After the Communists took over in 1944, Albania allied first with the Soviet Union (until 1960), and then with China (to 1978). In the early 1990s, Albania ended 46 years of Communist rule and established a multiparty democracy. Albania joined NATO and is a candidate for the European Union. Although Albania's economy continues to grow, the country is still one of the poorest in Eurasia.

Although Albania is a poor country, patrons still enjoy a visit to this café in Berat, Albania.

Follow the index every year at socialprogressimperative.org.
Quick Stats from CIA World Factbook.

EURASIAN COUNTRIES AT A GLANCE   **57**

A Syrian-Armenian mother and her son play in their apartment in Yerevan, Armenia. A century ago, Syria offered shelter to Armenian refugees, and in recent years Armenia became a haven for their descendants.

ARMENIA

QUICK STATS

Population: 3,056,382 (July 2015 est.)
Urban Population: 62.7% of total population (2015)
Comparative Size: slightly smaller than Maryland
Gross Domestic Product (per capita): $7,400 (2014 est.)
Gross Domestic Product (by sector): agriculture 21.9%, industry 31.5%, services 46.6% (2014 est.)
Government: republic
Languages: Armenian (official) 97.9%, Kurdish (spoken by Yezidi minority) 1%, other 1% (2011 est.)

SOCIAL PROGRESS SNAPSHOT

Social Progress Index: 65.70 (+4.70 above/below 61 world average)
Basic Human Needs: 82.60 (+14.27 above/below 68.33 world average)
Foundations of Well-being: 69.28 (+2.83 above/below 66.45 world average)
Opportunity: 45.24 (–2.99 above/below 48.23 world average)

Armenia prides itself on being the first nation to formally adopt Christianity (early fourth century). Despite periods of autonomy, over the centuries Armenia came under the sway of various empires. During World War I in the western portion of Armenia, the Ottoman Empire instituted a policy of forced resettlement coupled with other harsh practices that resulted in at least one million Armenian deaths. In January 2015 Armenia joined Russia, Belarus, and Kazakhstan as a member of the Eurasian Economic Union.

Shia and Sunni Muslim family members celebrate Eid al-Fitr, the festival that marks the end of the holy month of Ramadan, in Baku, Azerbaijan.

AZERBAIJAN

QUICK STATS

Population: 9,780,780 (July 2015 est.)
Urban Population: 62.7% of total population (2015)
Comparative Size: slightly smaller than Maine
Gross Domestic Product (per capita): $17,600 (2014 est.)
Gross Domestic Product (by sector): agriculture 5.7%, industry 61.2%, services 33.2% (2014 est.)
Government: republic
Languages: Azerbaijani (Azeri, official) 92.5%, Russian 1.4%, Armenian 1.4%, other 4.7% (2009 est.)

SOCIAL PROGRESS SNAPSHOT

Social Progress Index: 62.62 (+1.62 above/below 61 world average)
Basic Human Needs: 76.43 (+8.10 above/below 68.33 world average)
Foundations of Well-being: 68.03 (+1.58 above/below 66.45 world average)
Opportunity: 43.41 (–4.82 above/below 48.23 world average)

Oil-rich Azerbaijan is a Muslim-majority democratic and secular republic. It was incorporated into the Soviet Union for seven decades, until declaring independence in 1991. Armenia and Azerbaijan have been fighting over a disputed territory since 1988. Corruption in the country is widespread, and the government, which eliminated presidential term limits in 2009, has been accused of authoritarianism. Although poverty has been reduced and infrastructure investment has increased, reforms have not adequately addressed weaknesses in most government institutions.

A policeman passes protesters holding portraits of imprisoned and disappeared opposition activists during a "Day of Solidarity" in Minsk, Belarus. The fight for freedom and democracy is ongoing in Belarus.

BELARUS

QUICK STATS

Population: 9,589,689 (July 2015 est.)
Urban Population: 76.7% of total population (2015)
Comparative Size: slightly less than twice the size of Kentucky; slightly smaller than Kansas
Gross Domestic Product (per capita): $18,200 (2014 est.)
Gross Domestic Product (by sector): agriculture 7.3%, industry 37%, services 55.7% (2014 est.)
Government: republic in name, although in fact an authoritarian system centered on the executive
Languages: Russian (official) 70.2%, Belarusian (official) 23.4%, other 3.1% (includes small Polish- and Ukrainian-speaking minorities), unspecified 3.3% (2009 est.)

SOCIAL PROGRESS SNAPSHOT

Social Progress Index: 64.98 (+3.98 above/below 61 world average)
Basic Human Needs: 83.03 (+14.70 above/below 68.33 world average)
Foundations of Well-being: 66.72 (+0.27 above/below 66.45 world average)
Opportunity: 45.19 (–3.04 above/below 48.23 world average)

After seven decades as part of the Soviet Union, Belarus became independent in 1991. It has retained close political and economic ties to Russia. Belarus and Russia signed a treaty (1999) for greater political and economic integration. Since his election in 1994 as the country's first and only directly elected president, Alexander Lukashenko has steadily consolidated his power through authoritarian means. Government has restricted political and civil freedoms, freedom of speech and the press, peaceful assembly, and religion.

Citizens protest against unemployment, corruption, and privatization in Sarejevo, Bosnia and Herzegovina.

BOSNIA AND HERZEGOVINA

QUICK STATS

Population: 3,867,055 (July 2015 est.)
Urban Population: 39.8% of total population (2015)
Comparative Size: slightly smaller than West Virginia
Gross Domestic Product (per capita): $9,800 (2014 est.)
Gross Domestic Product (by sector): agriculture 8%, industry 26.3%, services 65.7% (2014 est.)
Government: republic in name, although in fact an authoritarian system centered on the executive
Languages: Bosnian (official), Croatian (official), Serbian (official)

SOCIAL PROGRESS SNAPSHOT

Social Progress Index: 66.15 (+5.15 above/below 61 world average)
Basic Human Needs: 85.78 (+17.45 above/below 68.33 world average)
Foundations of Well-being: 70.35 (+3.90 above/below 66.45 world average)
Opportunity: 42.33 (–5.90 above/below 48.23 world average)

Bosnia and Herzegovina declared independence from the former Yugoslavia in 1992 after a referendum boycotted by ethnic Serbs. The Bosnian Serbs responded with armed resistance aimed at partitioning the republic along ethnic lines. In 1995 warring parties agreed to a peace treaty that ended three years of interethnic strife. A multiethnic and democratic government was created. Also recognized was a second tier of government composed of two entities roughly equal in size: the Bosniak-Bosnian Croat Federation of Bosnia and Herzegovina and the Bosnian Serb-led Republika Srpska (RS).

Participants march during Alilo, a religious procession to celebrate Orthodox Christmas in the center of Tbilisi, Georgia.

GEORGIA

QUICK STATS

Population: 4,931,226 (July 2015 est.)
Urban Population: 53.6% of total population (2015)
Comparative Size: slightly smaller than South Carolina; slightly larger than West Virginia
Gross Domestic Product (per capita): $7,700 (2014 est.)
Gross Domestic Product (by sector): agriculture 9.1%, industry 21.8%, services 69.1% (2014 est.)
Government: republic
Languages: Georgian (official) 71%, Russian 9%, Armenian 7%, Azeri 6%, other 7%

SOCIAL PROGRESS SNAPSHOT

Social Progress Index: 65.89 (+4.89 above/below 61 world average)
Basic Human Needs: 80.15 (+11.82 above/below 68.33 world average)
Foundations of Well-being: 69.61 (+3.16 above/below 66.45 world average)
Opportunity: 47.92 (–0.31 above/below 48.23 world average)

Georgia was forcibly incorporated into the USSR in 1921 and regained its independence when the Soviet Union dissolved in 1991. Public discontent over corruption and ineffective government services, followed by an attempt to manipulate parliamentary elections in 2003, touched off protests that led to the resignation of president Eduard Shevardnadze. Georgia's recent elections show a former Soviet state that emerged to conduct democratic and peaceful government transitions of power. Popular and government support for integration with the West is high.

Young Macedonians enjoy a peace concert in Tetovo, Macedonia.

MACEDONIA

QUICK STATS

Population: 2,096,015 (July 2015 est.)
Urban Population: 57.1% of total population (2015)
Comparative Size: slightly larger than Vermont
Gross Domestic Product (per capita): $13,300 (2014 est.)
Gross Domestic Product (by sector): agriculture 8.8%, industry 21.3%, services 69.9% (2014 est.)
Government: parliamentary democracy
Languages: Macedonian (official) 66.5%, Albanian (official) 25.1%, Turkish 3.5%, Roma 1.9%, Serbian 1.2%, other 1.8% (2002 est.)

SOCIAL PROGRESS SNAPSHOT

Social Progress Index: 67.79 (+6.79 above/below 61 world average)
Basic Human Needs: 83.53 (+15.20 above/below 68.33 world average)
Foundations of Well-being: 67.04 (+0.59 above/below 66.45 world average)
Opportunity: 52.80 (+4.57 above/below 48.23 world average)

Macedonia gained its independence peacefully from Yugoslavia in 1991. In 1995 Greece lifted a 20-month trade embargo, and the two countries agreed to normalize relations, but the use of the country's Hellenic name remains a problem with Greece, and negotiations for a solution are ongoing. Ethnic Albanian grievances over perceived political and economic inequities escalated into an insurgency in 2001 that eventually led to an internationally brokered peace agreement. Macedonia became an EU candidate in 2005.

Dancers perform during the opening ceremony of the National Wine Festival in Moldova.

MOLDOVA

QUICK STATS

Population: 3,546,847 (July 2015 est.)
Urban Population: 45% of total population (2015)
Comparative Size: slightly larger than Maryland
Gross Domestic Product (per capita): $5,000 (2014 est.)
Gross Domestic Product (by sector): agriculture 15.7%, industry 20%, services 64.3% (2014 est.)
Government: republic
Language(s): Moldovan 58.8% (official; virtually the same as the Romanian language), Romanian 16.4%, Russian 16%, Ukrainian 3.8%, Gagauz 3.1% (a Turkish language), Bulgarian 1.1%, other 0.3%, unspecified 0.4%

SOCIAL PROGRESS SNAPSHOT

Social Progress Index: 63.68 (+2.68 above/below 61 world average)
Basic Human Needs: 77.65 (+9.32 above/below 68.33 world average)
Foundations of Well-being: 64.85 (–1.60 above/below 66.45 world average)
Opportunity: 48.54 (+0.31 above/below 48.23 world average)

Once part of Romania, Moldova was incorporated into the Soviet Union after World War II. Although independent from the USSR since 1991, Russian forces have remained in Moldovan territory supporting the separatist region of Transnistria, composed of a Slavic majority population (mostly Ukrainians and Russians). Europe's poorest economy, Moldova became the first former Soviet state to elect a Communist, Vladimir Voronin, as its president in 2001. Moldova has parliamentary elections, and the president is directly elected by parliament.

Many tourists visit the charming town of Perast, Montenegro.

MONTENEGRO

QUICK STATS

Population: 647,073 (July 2015 est.)
Urban Population: 64% of total population (2015)
Comparative Size: slightly smaller than Connecticut
Gross Domestic Product (per capita): $15,000 (2014 est.)
Gross Domestic Product (by sector): agriculture 8.3%, industry 21.2%, services 70.5% (2013 est.)
Government: republic
Languages: Serbian 42.9%, Montenegrin (official) 37%, Bosnian 5.3%, Albanian 5.3%, Serbo-Croat 2%, other 3.5%, unspecified 4% (2011 est.)

SOCIAL PROGRESS SNAPSHOT

Social Progress Index: 69.01 (+8.01 above/below 61 world average)
Basic Human Needs: 81.89 (+13.56 above/below 68.33 world average)
Foundations of Well-being: 72.09 (+5.64 above/below 66.45 world average)
Opportunity: 53.04 (+4.81 above/below 48.23 world average)

The use of the name Black Mountain (Montenegro) began in the 1200s. Montenegro was recognized as an independent principality in 1878. After World War I, Montenegro was absorbed by the kingdom that became Yugoslavia in 1929; after World War II, it became a republic of Yugoslavia. When Yugoslavia broke up in 1992, Montenegro joined with Serbia to form the Federal Republic of Yugoslavia. In May 2006 a referendum on independence allowed Montenegro to formally restore its independence from Serbia. It is a candidate for the European Union and in December 2015 was invited to join NATO.

Russian families enjoy using outdoor ice slides and winter themed activities during the winter in Ufa, Russia.

RUSSIA

QUICK STATS

Population: 142,423,773 (July 2015 est.)
Urban Population: 74% of total population (2015)
Comparative Size: approximately 1.8 times the size of the United States
Gross Domestic Product (per capita): $24,800 (2014 est.)
Gross Domestic Product (by sector): agriculture 9.7%, industry 27.8%, services 62.5% (2012)
Government: federation
Languages: Russian (official) 96.3%, Dolgang 5.3%, German 1.5%, Chechen 1%, Tatar 3%, other 10.3%

SOCIAL PROGRESS SNAPSHOT

Social Progress Index: 63.64 (+2.64 above/below 61 world average)
Basic Human Needs: 74.10 (+5.77 above/below 68.33 world average)
Foundations of Well-being: 67.63 (+1.18 above/below 66.45 world average)
Opportunity: 49.19 (+0.96 above/below 48.23 world average)

In 1917 the Communists under Vladimir Lenin overthrew the tsar and formed the Union of Soviet Socialist Republics (USSR), or the Soviet Union. Joseph Stalin's brutal rule (1928–1953) strengthened Russian dominance of the Soviet Union but cost tens of millions of lives. The economy and culture stagnated for decades until General Secretary Mikhail Gorbachev (1985–1991) introduced glasnost (openness) and perestroika (restructuring). His initiatives inadvertently led to the Soviet Union splintering into Russia and 14 other independent republics. Following economic and political turmoil under President Boris Yeltsin (1991–1999), Russia shifted toward a centralized semi-authoritarian state under President Vladimir Putin.

Contestants battle at a festival of knighthood in Despotovac, Serbia.

SERBIA

QUICK STATS

Population: 7,176,794
Urban Population: 55.6% of total population (2015)
Comparative Size: slightly smaller than South Carolina
Gross Domestic Product (per capita): $13,300 (2014 est.)
Gross Domestic Product (by sector): agriculture 8.2%, industry 36.9%, services 54.9% (2014 est.)
Government: republic
Languages: Serbian (official) 88.1%, Hungarian 3.4%, Bosnian 1.9%, Romany 1.4%, other 3.4%, undeclared or unknown 1.8%

SOCIAL PROGRESS SNAPSHOT

Social Progress Index: 69.79 (+8.79 above/below 61 world average)
Basic Human Needs: 83.38 (+15.05 above/below 68.33 world average)
Foundations of Well-being: 74.74 (+8.29 above/below 66.45 world average)
Opportunity: 51.25 (+3.02 above/below 48.23 world average)

The Kingdom of Serbs, Croats, and Slovenes was formed in 1918; its name was changed to Yugoslavia in 1929. After World War II, the Communist regime of Josip Broz Tito took full control. In 1989 Slobodan Milosevic's ultranationalist calls for Serbian domination led to the violent breakup of Yugoslavia along ethnic lines. In 1991 Croatia, Slovenia, and Macedonia declared independence, followed by Bosnia in 1992. In 2006 Montenegro broke away from Serbia, followed by Kosovo, although Serbia has not recognized Kosovo's independence. In 2014 the European Union opened formal negotiations on Serbia's membership in the EU.

The Grand Bazaar in Istanbul, Turkey, is one of the largest and oldest covered markets in the world, with 61 covered streets and more than 3,000 shops.

TURKEY

QUICK STATS

Population: 79,414,269 (July 2015 est.)
Urban Population: 73.4% of total population (2015)
Comparative Size: slightly larger than Texas
Gross Domestic Product (per capita): $19,600 (2014 est.)
Gross Domestic Product (by sector): agriculture 8.2%, industry 26.9%. services 64.9% (2014 est.)
Languages: Turkish (official), Kurdish, other minority languages

SOCIAL PROGRESS SNAPSHOT

Social Progress Index: 66.24 (+5.24 above/below 61 world average)
Basic Human Needs: 81.50 (+13.17 above/below 68.33 world average)
Foundations of Well-being: 66.61 (+.16 above/below 66.45 world average)
Opportunity: 50.61 (+2.38 above/below 48.23 world average)

Founded in 1923 by Mustafa Kemal Atatürk, modern Turkey adopted social, legal, and political reforms. Since then, Turkish political parties have multiplied, but democracy has been fractured by intermittent military coups. Turkey has acted as patron state to the "Turkish Republic of Northern Cyprus." A Kurdish insurgency begun in 1984 claimed more than 30,000 lives. In 1999 insurgents largely withdrew from Turkey. Turkey joined the United Nations (1945) and NATO (1952) and started EU membership talks in 2005. Recent economic reforms have contributed to a growing economy.

Ukrainians take part in the Ukrainian Global Climate March.

UKRAINE

QUICK STATS

Population: 44,429,471 (July 2015 est.)

Urban Population: 69.7% of total population (2015)

Comparative Size: almost four times the size of Georgia; slightly smaller than Texas

Gross Domestic Product (per capita): $8,700 (2014 est.)

Gross Domestic Product (by sector): agriculture 12.1%, industry 29%, services 58.8% (2014 est.)

Government: republic

Languages: Ukrainian (official) 67.5%, Russian (regional language) 29.6%, other (includes small Crimean Tatar-, Moldavian-, and Hungarian-speaking minorities) 2.9% (2001 est.)

SOCIAL PROGRESS SNAPSHOT

Social Progress Index: 65.69 (+4.69 above/below 61 world average)

Basic Human Needs: 78.28 (+9.95 above/below 68.33 world average)

Foundations of Well-being: 61.74 (–4.71 above/below 66.45 world average)

Opportunity: 57.05 (+8.82 above/below 48.23 world average)

Shortly after the collapse of tsarist Russia in 1917, Ukraine endured a Soviet rule that led to two forced famines (1921–1922 and 1932–1933) in which over eight million people died. In World War II, German and Soviet armies were responsible for seven to eight million more deaths. Although Ukraine achieved independence in 1991, democracy and prosperity remained elusive. A peaceful mass protest in 2004 forced authorities to overturn a rigged presidential election. A new internationally monitored vote brought reformist Viktor Yushchenko to power. When Viktor Yanukovych became president in 2010, he strengthened ties with Russia. After pro-West Petro Poroshenko became president in 2014, Russian president Vladimir Putin ordered the invasion of Ukraine's Crimean peninsula, claiming the action was to protect ethnic Russians there. Russia illegally annexed Crimea after a "referendum" and continues to support a separatist movement in eastern Ukraine.

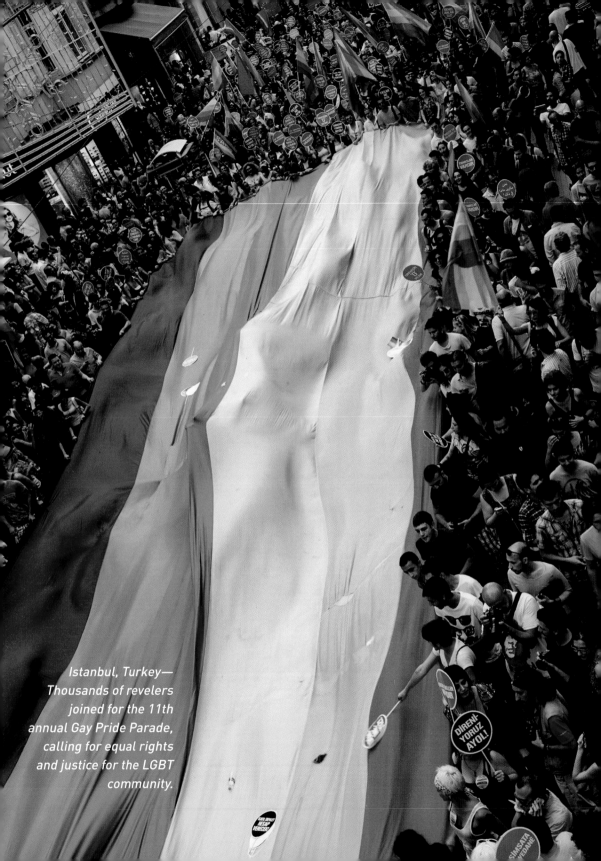

Istanbul, Turkey—
Thousands of revelers
joined for the 11th
annual Gay Pride Parade,
calling for equal rights
and justice for the LGBT
community.

Conclusion

Eurasia is entering a time of great changes. The 1990s brought a period of upheaval during which many countries that were under Soviet control became independent. Western influence led many newly formed governments to become more democratic, establishing political rule by elected officials. Several countries that were controlled by Russia have now aligned themselves with the European Union. While Russia started the 1990s heading toward more Western ideals and freedoms, President Vladimir Putin has taken steps away from establishing more freedoms and connections with the West. He has solidified his authoritarian control of the country and turned toward the East, establishing a genuine strategic partnership with China. A Eurasian Economic Union has been put together to build economic unity and prosperity in the region. Although change may be slow, the past few decades have brought expanded personal freedoms and improved quality of life for increasing numbers of citizens throughout Eurasia. The influence of the global free market system and the Internet have led to more sharing of cultural insight and knowledge throughout the world. In Turkey, a secular state continues with free elections. In recent years, President Recep Tayyip Erdogan, an Islamist, has tightened his control over the country (cracking down on any sort of criticism of his policies), but his party lost a majority in Parliament after a vote in the summer of 2015. In summary, the countries of Eurasia and their people have advanced in the past 50 years toward conditions that improve quality of life and provide more personal freedoms.

Mothers and pregnant women in Chisinau, Moldova, attend a protest against a government reduction in allowances for working mothers.

Series Glossary

Anemia: a condition in which the blood doesn't have enough healthy red blood cells, most often caused by not having enough iron

Aquifer: an underground layer of water-bearing permeable rock, from which groundwater can be extracted using a water well

Asylum: protection granted by a nation to someone who has left their native country as a political refugee

Basic human needs: the things people need to stay alive: clean water, sanitation, food, shelter, basic medical care, safety

Biodiversity: the variety of life that is absolutely essential to the health of different ecosystems

Carbon dioxide (CO₂): a greenhouse gas that contributes to global warming and climate change

Censorship: the practice of officially examining books, movies, and other media and art, and suppressing unacceptable parts

Child mortality rate: the number of children that die before their fifth birthday for every 1,000 babies born alive

Communicable diseases: medical conditions spread by airborne viruses or bacteria or through bodily fluids such as malaria, tuberculosis, and HIV/AIDS; also called **infectious diseases;** differ from **noncommunicable diseases**, medical conditions not caused by infection and requiring long-term treatment such as diabetes or heart disease

Contraception: any form of birth control used to prevent pregnancy

Corruption: the dishonest behavior by people in positions of power for their own benefit

Deforestation: the clearing of trees, transforming a forest into cleared land

Desalination: a process that removes minerals (including salt) from ocean water

Discrimination: the unjust or prejudicial treatment of different categories of people, especially on the grounds of race, age, or sex

Ecosystem: a biological community of interacting organisms and their physical environment

Ecosystem sustainability: when we care for resources like clean air, water, plants, and animals so that they will be available to future generations

Emissions: the production and discharge of something, especially gas or radiation

Ethnicities: social groups that have a common national or cultural tradition

Extremism: the holding of extreme political or religious views; fanaticism

Famine: a widespread scarcity of food that results in malnutrition and starvation on a large scale

Food desert: a neighborhood or community with no walking access to affordable, nutritious food

Food security: having enough to eat at all times

Greenhouse gas emissions: any of the atmospheric gases that contribute to the greenhouse effect by absorbing infrared radiation produced by solar warming of the earth's surface. They include carbon dioxide (CO_2), methane (CH_4), nitrous oxide (NO_2), and water vapor.

Gross domestic product (GDP): the total value of all products and services created in a country during a year

GDP per capita (per person): the gross domestic product divided by the number of people in the country. For example, if the GDP for a country is one hundred million dollars ($100,000,000) and the population is one million people (1,000,000), then the GDP per capita (value created per person) is $100.

Habitat: environment for a plant or animal, including climate, food, water, and shelter

Incarceration: the condition of being imprisoned

Income inequality: when the wealth of a country is spread very unevenly among the population

Indigenous people: culturally distinct groups with long-standing ties to the land in a specific area

Inflation: when the same amount money buys less from one day to the next. Just because things cost more does not mean that people have more money. Low-income people trapped in a high inflation economy can quickly find themselves unable to purchase even the basics like food.

Infrastructure: permanent features required for an economy to operate such as transportation routes and electric grids; also systems such as education and courts

Latrine: a communal outdoor toilet, such as a trench dug in the ground

Literate: able to read and write

Malnutrition: lack of proper nutrition, caused by not having enough to eat, not eating enough of the right things, or being unable to use the food that one does eat

Maternal mortality rate: the number of pregnant women who die for every 100,000 births.

Natural resources: industrial materials and assets provided by nature such as metal deposits, timber, and water

Nongovernmental organization (NGO): a nonprofit, voluntary citizens' group organized on a local, national, or international level. Examples include organizations that support human rights, advocate for political participation, and work for improved health care.

Parliament: a group of people who are responsible for making the laws in some kinds of government

Prejudice: an opinion that isn't based on facts or reason

Preventive care: health care that helps an individual avoid illness

Primary school: includes grades 1–6 (also known as elementary school); precedes **secondary** and **tertiary education**, schooling beyond the primary grades; secondary generally corresponds to high school, and tertiary generally means college-level

Privatization: the transfer of ownership, property, or business from the government to the private sector (the part of the national economy that is not under direct government control)

Sanitation: conditions relating to public health, especially the provision of clean drinking water and adequate sewage disposal

Stereotypes: are common beliefs about the nature of the members of a specific group that are based on limited experience or incorrect information

Subsistence agriculture: a system of farming that supplies the needs of the farm family without generating any surplus for sale

Surface water: the water found above ground in streams, lakes, and rivers

Tolerance: a fair, objective, and permissive attitude toward those whose opinions, beliefs, practices, racial or ethnic origins, and so on differ from one's own

Trafficking: dealing or trading in something illegal

Transparency: means that the government operates in a way that is visible to and understood by the public

Universal health care: a system in which every person in a country has access to doctors and hospitals

Urbanization: the process by which towns and cities are formed and become larger as more and more people begin living and working in central areas

Well-being: the feeling people have when they are healthy, comfortable, and happy

Whistleblower: someone who reveals private information about the illegal activities of a person or organization

NDALOHET MBULIMI I MENDJES, E JO I KOKËS

Hundreds of Muslims gathered in downtown Pristina, Kosovo, to protest against the Kosovo government's decision to ban headscarves in schools.

Index

alcoholism, 23, 24, 25, 26, 38, 40

basic human needs, 23-30

censorship, 33, 36

communications, access to, 36

    Internet, 25, 36, 37, 71

corruption, 12, 46, 54, 60

democracy, 19, 45, 46, 48, 59, 71

disease, 27

economy, 12, 13, 15, 19, 20, 38

ecosystems, 33, 41

education, 12, 19, 33, 34, 35, 41, 48, 54

education, higher, 48

environment, 12, 40, 41, 44

freedoms, 19, 29, 45, 46, 48, 49, 51,
    53, 54, 71

foundations of well-being, 33-42

government, 12, 14, 15, 18, 19, 21, 24, 25, 26,
    35, 36, 38, 41, 44, 46, 49, 51, 69, 72, 75

health, 12, 23, 24, 25, 27, 54

    health care, 23, 25, 26, 27

    infant mortality, 27

    maternal health, 26, 27

housing, 23, 28, 29

immigrants, 48

income inequality, 20

industrialization, 12, 18, 33, 41

LGBT rights, 48, 49, 51, 54, 70

life expectancy, 38

literacy, 16, 33

medical care, 12, 23

military, 14, 15, 18, 38

minorities, 35

nutrition, 12, 23, 25

obesity, 38

opportunity, 45-54

pollution, 40, 41

poverty, 20, 25

protest, 36, 44, 50, 51, 59, 60, 72, 76

Putin, Vladimir, 15, 20, 26, 28, 46, 47, 51, 71

reform, 17, 49

refugees, 15, 22

religion, 11, 16, 21, 35, 48, 54

rights, 12, 18, 35, 45, 46, 48, 49, 51, 53, 54, 70

sanitation, 30

shelter, 22

social progress, in Eurasia (overview), 11

tolerance, 48

employment, 12, 54, 60

violence, 15, 54

vote, 14, 47, 71

    free elections, 46, 53, 71

water, 30, 40, 41

A girl lo
through
broken wind
of her ho
in Sko
Macedo
Around 14.
Macedor
families rece
state social
from 30 to
euros per fa
per mo

RESOURCES

Continue exploring the world of development through this assortment of online and print resources. Follow links, stay organized, and maintain a critical perspective. Also, seek out news sources from outside the country in which you live.

Websites

Social Progress Imperative: socialprogressimperative.org

United Nations—Human Development Indicators: hdr.undp.org/en/countries and Sustainable Development Goals: un.org/sustainabledevelopment/sustainable-development-goals

World Bank—World Development Indicators: data.worldbank.org/data-catalog/world-development-indicators

World Health Organization—country statistics: who.int/gho/countries/en

U.S. State Department—human rights tracking site: humanrights.gov/dyn/countries.html

Oxfam International: oxfam.org/en

Amnesty International: amnesty.org/en

Human Rights Watch: hrw.org

Reporters without Borders: en.rsf.org

CIA—The World Factbook: cia.gov/library/publications/the-world-factbook

Books

Literary and classics

The Good Earth, Pearl S. Buck

Grapes of Wrath, John Steinbeck

The Jungle, Upton Sinclair

Nonfiction—historical/classic

Angela's Ashes, Frank McCourt

Lakota Woman, Mary Crow Dog with Richard Erdoes

Orientalism, Edward Said

Silent Spring, Rachel Carson

The Souls of Black Folk, W.E.B. Du Bois

Nonfiction: development and policy—presenting a range of views

Behind the Beautiful Forevers: Life, Death, and Hope in a Mumbai Undercity, Katherine Boo

The Bottom Billion: Why the Poorest Countries Are Failing and What Can Be Done About It, Paul Collier

The End of Poverty, Jeffrey D. Sachs

For the Common Good: Redirecting the Economy toward Community, the Environment, and a Sustainable Future, Herman E. Daly

I Am Malala: The Girl Who Stood Up for Education and Was Shot by the Taliban, Malala Yousafzai and Christina Lamb

The Life You Can Save: Acting Now to End World Poverty, Peter Singer

Mismeasuring Our Lives: Why GDP Doesn't Add Up, Joseph E. Stiglitz, Amartya Sen, and Jean-Paul Fitoussi

Rachel and Her Children: Homeless Families in America, Jonathan Kozol

The White Man's Burden: Why the West's Efforts to Aid the Rest Have Done So Much Ill and So Little Good, William Easterly

Foreword writer Michael Green is an economist, author, and cofounder of the Social Progressive Imperative. A UK native and graduate of Oxford University, Green has worked in aid and development for the British government and taught economics at Warsaw University.

Author Don Rauf has written more than 30 nonfiction books, mostly for children and young adults, including *Killer Lipstick and Other Spy Gadgets*, *The Rise and Fall of the Ottoman Empire*, and *Simple Rules for Card Games*. He lives in Seattle with his wife, Monique, and son, Leo.